Shrewsbury
Then and Now

Photographs from the Shropshire Records and Research Unit

Shropshire Books

Front Cover: Mardol. Painting by Thomas Shotter Boys 1858.
Reproduced courtesy of Shrewsbury Museum Service

ISBN 0-903802-49-X © Shropshire Records and Research Unit 1991
Cover and book design: Daywell Designs
Published by Shropshire Books, Shropshire County Council's Leisure Services Department
Printed in Great Britain by Livesey Limited

Introduction

Shrewsbury is promoted as a quaint medieval and Tudor town to encourage tourists to visit, but it is really a thriving late twentieth century community which operates in a townscape which happens to contain many relics of the past. Its street plan, its houses, shops and public buildings are in many instances ancient, but they have only survived because they suited, or could be made to suit, changing modern requirements. Such adjustments, the balancing of present need with sentimental attachment to the outmoded, must have been required constantly in the town's history; it is our good fortune that so much that is appealing to us from the past has survived. Change must always be regarded with suspicion, but some change is inevitable if an ancient town is to meet the pressing new demands placed upon it.

These photographs reveal some of the alterations which have occurred in Shrewsbury in the last two hundred years. How you regard them is a matter of personal opinion. The book's intention is to remind those who can remember and inform those who cannot of some of the changes that have taken place. If it encourages any reader to research the reasons for change in this local context the staff of the Records and Research Unit in Shrewsbury will be pleased to assist them. If any reader has any old photographs which they wish to donate or which they will allow to be copied, the staff would be delighted to hear from them.

All the new photographs were taken in September 1991. Precise dates of the old views are unknown in some cases. It has not always been possible to take the modern photograph from the exact position of the old and the different specifications of the old camera lenses has meant that some pairs of illustrations are less precisely similar than they might have been, however, the hope is that by comparing the two views the reader can detect the subtle changes which have taken place.

1.   Chester Street in 1938 a year before the buildings on the left side were demolished for road widening. At this time they housed the Swan Hotel, a butcher's, a delicensed hotel (the Greyhound), a tailor's, fruiterer's, house agent and builders' suppliers. Behind them were yards containing several cramped houses.

2. Chester Street in 1991. Road widening has recurred here recently making this one of the busiest road junctions in the town. The achitecturally eccentric building on the right remains to provide a reference point between the old and new views.

3. Howard Street c1898. The Eagle Hotel was less than seventy years old when this photograph was taken but was about to be demolished to make way for the enlargement of the railway station. Beyond it lay the Lilleshall Company's coal, lime and brick depot and the railway warehouses of T.Southam and Sons wine and spirit importers of Wyle Cop.

4. Howard Street 1991. Southam's warehouse, slightly rebuilt, remains and is called the Buttermarket, but the line of the original street has been covered by the extended station.

5. Severn Viaduct April 1894. This handsome stone bridge was built to carry the Shrewsbury to Birmingham railway line opened in 1849. Beyond it can be seen St Mary's church spire still lacking its topmost section which had blown down a few weeks earlier.

6. Severn Viaduct 1991. The massive reconstruction of the station around 1900 involved the widening of the river crossing; two additional iron bridges were built on either side of the stone bridge.

7. Station c1905. The rebuilt station still reveals patches of clean white Grinshill stone showing where it was altered. The Raven cab carried guests the short distance between the hotel in Castle Street and the station without having to follow any one way system. The varied headgear of the passers-by reveals their social status.

8. Station 1991. Apart from the vehicles, little has changed, but Shrewsbury, once a major railway centre appears to be about to lose its through train services to London.

9. School Gardens 1791 showing the County Gaol of 1705. The building was by this date congested as criminals could no longer be transported to the American Colonies. The new prison in Howard Street replaced this gaol in 1793.

10. School Gardens 1991. The Queen Anne building is still recognisable but is now divided into flats and offices. The prison exercise yard has become a car park.

11. Castle Street c1880. The gas lamp has the street name on its glass but this view is difficult to recognise as several buildings have been demolished or rebuilt. The impressive timber-framed house opposite the Library, which is such an ornament to this end of the town, was still covered in plaster at this time.

12. Castle Street 1991. A place of grinding gears, petrol and diesel fumes and almost incessant traffic.

13. Pride Hill / St Mary's Street c1870. The Butter Market as rebuilt in 1844. The Street at the top of Pride Hill had long been the place where dairy produce was sold; the medieval High Cross, which stood here (on High Pavement) until 1705, would have been the focus for this important trade .

14. Pride Hill / St Mary's Street 1991. This corner has been occupied by the town's main Post Office since 1875 but the adjoining premises have only recently become 'fast food' outlets.

15. Pride Hill 1903. The shops are tightly shuttered so this photograph was probably taken on a Sunday. The painted canvas or wooden archway was just one of many which were put up around the town whenever sufficient excuse was found; in this case the arch and the flags further down the hill were to celebrate the five hundredth anniversary of the Battle of Shrewsbury.

16. Pride Hill 1991. Since 1982 pedestrians have had, in theory, this pleasant street to themselves through the greater part of the day.

17. Butcher Row 1893. On the right we can see a display of baskets in the open shop front of Mr A. Munslow basket maker. Next door, a young woman from the Rising Sun Inn is curious about the photographer. This short street was still home to many families; in the 1881 census 135 people were listed as resident in the Row.

18. Butcher Row 1991. Virtually all the buildings on the right have been altered and those at the end of the street have been demolished. Only a dozen or so people now live here.

19. St Alkmund's Place c1940. Here we see the other side of the buildings seen at the end of Butcher Row in 17.
St Alkmund's churchyard still had its iron railings beyond which can be glimpsed a passage beneath the word "Linoleums";
this was known as Burying or Burial Shut as it led straight to the gates of the graveyard .

20. St Alkmund's Place 1991. Apart from the horse chestnut tree, now much larger, nothing remains of the earlier view.

21. Fish Street c1912. Walker's printing offices occupied the building on the right hand side of Grope Lane as you walk down to High Street. The printing presses in the basement must have been deafening in this confined space. The staff have left off their work for this photograph to be taken. A shiny motor car can be seen on the far right; did this carry Mr. Walker back to his home at the Brooklands in Meole Brace at the end of the day?

22. Fish Street 1991. The scene is almost unchanged, even the roadway is the same, but this photograph exemplifies the huge changes that have occurred in both the types of businesses and the number of people employed in the town centre. The small light industrial workshops employing 30-40 people which were to be found in most parts of central Shrewsbury have long gone.

23. High Street c1883. These premises were called the Cross Keys but had also been named the Globe from 1780 to 1820. Mr. H. F. Newman, a Wellington man, "devoted special attention to ale and stout bottling" and "finds no difficulty in meeting all demands in the promptest style". He also "makes a special feature of that celebrated sherry Vino de Pasto at 3s 4d the single bottle and 40s the dozen."

24. High Street 1991. The building has been restored and altered recently after a period of neglect. The restorers have added a number of contemporary allusions in the new carvings for the amusement of observant viewers.

25. The Square c1890 dominated by the Shirehall designed by Sir Robert Smirke in 1833. The interior of the building had been rebuilt after a serious fire in 1880. In the distance on the right can be seen the distinctive roof of the Workingmens Hall, a Victorian institution intended to provide an alternative non-alcoholic meeting place for men who would otherwise go to pubs.

26. The Square 1991. The old Shirehall building was demolished in 1971 and was replaced by a modern structure containing offices, shops and car park.

27. The Square c1928. Parking had not yet become a major problem in Shrewsbury; you could even leave your horse and
carriage outside Grocott's shop while bargain hunting at the Sale.

28. The Square 1991. Cars are no longer encouraged to linger in this area which has become increasingly pedestrianised in the last decade. Though the buildings are the same, their uses have changed completely.

29. The Square 1902 shows an Elizabethan draper's house, Lloyd's Mansion, decorated to mark the return of Shropshire soldiers from the Boer War. The building was then part of Della Porta's shop.

30. The Square 1991. The timber-framed building was demolished c1930 to make way for an extension of the Shirehall which was itself demolished in 1971.

OLD MARKET HALL, SHREWSBURY

JUDGES LTD

31. The Square c1928. The view is dominated by the Market Hall and Lloyd's Mansion which were both expressions of Shrewsbury's civic pride in the reign of Elizabeth I.

32. The Square 1991. The Market Hall remains, but a piece of architecture of the reign of Elizabeth II now occupies the site of Lloyd's Mansion.

33. Mardol Head c1868. These unusual buildings stood at the top of Mardol until they were demolished prior to the construction of the General Market. They are seen in their pride on the cover of this book.

34. Mardol Head 1991. The site is now occupied by widened roadway, a flower bed and an almost featureless concrete wall.

35. Claremont Street c1867. The Baptist chapel stood behind the brick wall and heavy iron gates on the right. To the annoyance of late risers, queues of chattering Salopians formed early each morning to draw water at the pump, one of the few in this neighbourhood. The timber-framed building later became a public house called the Mermaid.

36. Claremont Street 1991. The rebuilt chapel survives but every other building has disappeared or been transformed as part of the Barker Street clearance of c1932.

37. Bellstone c1867. Demolition on the scale needed to clear the General Market site had probably not taken place since the years immediately after the Norman Conquest when 51 dwellings were razed to make way for the castle. This encouraged local photographers to make an extensive record of the project. Here we see the heaps of brick and rubble at the junction of Claremont Street and Bellstone.

38. Bellstone 1991. Apart from the much altered Theatre building of 1833, now a shop, nothing survives of the earlier view.

39. Bellstone c1930. On the right is the corner of the market building completed in 1869 which contained the Corn Exchange which explains the name of the public house in the photograph. All of the buildings on the left hand side of the street were to be demolished a few years later.

40. Bellstone 1991. The street widening of 1935 removed all the buildings on this side of the street, but, remarkably, the frontages of some were rebuilt on the new alignment.

41. St John's Hill / Shoplatch 1931. Two grandiose nineteenth century buildings, the General Market and the Theatre Royal gave this part of town a distinction of its own. The theatre/cinema built on the site of one of the town's most magnificent medieval stone houses, Charlton Hall, suffered a major fire in 1945 and closed as a place of entertainment soon after.

42. St John's Hill / Shoplatch 1991. The new market building of 1963 now dominates the view. It houses the lively weekday and Saturday markets at which local traders from many miles around sell their produce direct to the public.

43. Hill's Lane cl910. These picturesque crumbling buildings were in Ship Inn Yard, but they were in reality unhealthy tenement slums. Rowley's mansion can be seen to the left.

44. Hill's Lane 1991. Rowley's House and Mansion were restored as the town's archaeological museum when the slum dwellings around them were demolished in the 1930's. The open space that was created was used as a car park and bus station but plans now exist to redevelop the site.

45. Barker Street / Bridge Street c1937. This rather forbidding building was part of St Chad's School built in 1838-9 for the education of the poor of the parish of whom there were a large number; it closed in 1936.

46. Barker Street / Bridge Street 1991. A busy road junction has replaced the main school building. The school house survives and has been used as a refuge for homeless men.

47. Frankwell 1869. Local photographers have always been stimulated to record the unaccustomed presence of the muddy brown River Severn in the streets of the lower lying parts of town; this was one of the earliest floods to be photographed. Apart from the water and some bemused local inhabitants interested in the two novelties, a flood and a camera, this view shows that the timber-framed buildings in Frankwell were often concealed by plaster as they were throughout the town.

48. Frankwell 1991. For centuries Frankwell was a densely populated community many of whose members worked in connection with Shrewsbury's important river trade. Now few people live in the older part of the suburb, but its old buildings still contain several long-established thriving shops.

49. Welsh Bridge c1895. On the left bank, immediately below the chimney of the Circus Brewery, is Mardol Quay. On the opposite bank, out of the picture, is Frankwell Quay. Both of these had been important loading and unloading points for centuries before the town's river traffic petered out in the nineteenth century. They formerly lay below the medieval Welsh Bridge, the town abutment of which is marked by the single storey brick building with a sloping roof on the left.

50. Welsh Bridge 1991. Both banks of the river have been tidied up and planted. Few reminders of the centuries of commercial activity which took place here remain.

51. Frankwell 1947? This picture shows how local people coped with floods; a one way foot traffic system is in operation with a build-up of pedestrians waiting their turn to come into town over the makeshift bridges.

52. Frankwell 1991. Some of the buildings have been replaced but many remain. Appreciating them is made difficult by the incessant traffic.

53. Frankwell c1905. This view shows a splendid collection of sixteenth to nineteenth century buildings, but fails to hint at the squalid housing conditions of those who lived in the many courtyards leading off the street.

54. Frankwell 1991. Many of the frontages remain but the overcrowded alleys have been demolished.

55. Frankwell c1900. The timber-framed building was built in 1576-7, probably as a private house, but had become a public house by 1786.

56. Frankwell 1991. The String of Horses Inn and the adjoining buildings were demolished to make a traffic roundabout in the 1960s. The inn building was reconstructed at Avoncroft Museum in Worcestershire.

57. New Street 1965. The **String of Horses** building shortly before its demolition and removal.

58. New Street 1991. At busy times even the traffic roundabout cannot cope with the volume of traffic.

59. Frankwell 1963. All of these buildings were due for demolition to make way for the new traffic island. A narrow street, Chapel Street, can be seen at the end of the row of cottages; it led to the little Methodist chapel in New Street.

60. Frankwell 1991.

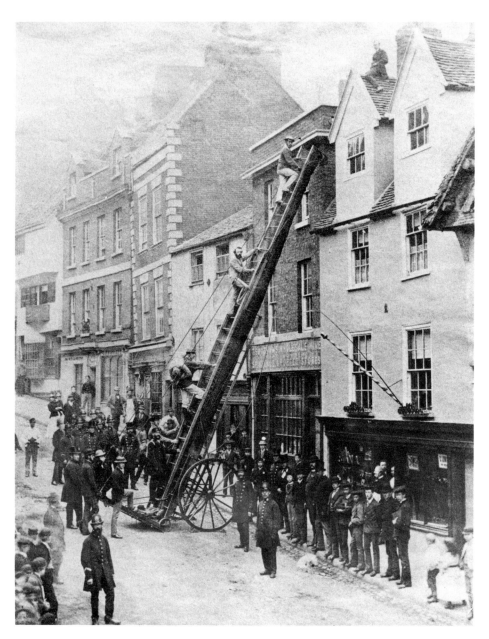

61 Wyle Cop c1875. It is not known
who these men were or whose ladder
this was, but their demonstration of
its properties clearly drew a large
crowd of policemen and schoolboys.

62. Wyle Cop 1991.
   The buildings are the same as those
   shown in the nineteenth century
   photograph though some have been
   stripped of plaster to reveal
   their timber-framing. Only one shop
   front has survived unchanged.

63. Wyle Cop cl870.
   The photographic apparatus on its
   tripod standing in the roadway has
   caught the attention of all the people
   on the street.

64. Wyle Cop 1991.
   It is no longer possible to stand in the road to take a photograph!

65. Abbey Gardens c1905. The buildings on the left housed the Shrewsbury Technical School. The gardens, formerly a stone yard belonging to the builder and architect John Carline, contained abandoned pieces of sculpture from local buildings. Wilfred Owen attended this school from 1907 to 1911.

66. Abbey Gardens 1991. New school buildings were constructed on this site in 1936. The gardens remain a peaceful retreat and a fine vantage point from which to observe the many wild birds which live on or by the river.

67. Abbey Foregate 1906. The Abbey water mill had had nearly eight centuries of active use before becoming a builders' store and timber yard; this burned with spectacular effect, in the middle of the night in August 1906 threatening to ignite the scaffolding surrounding the Abbey church which was being restored.

68. Abbey Foregate 1991. Part of the site has recently been buried under a new road scheme, but some medieval monastic remains still stand awaiting restoration.

69. Abbey Foregate 1899. Here we see the curate from the Abbey, Rev W.B. McNab, distributing soup and paraffin to marooned parishioners by the Abbey church.

70. Abbey Foregate 1991.

71. Abbey Foregate c1927. This waste ground had been turned into the stone yard, complete with masons' lodge next to the large house, for the major engineering task of rebuilding and widening the English Bridge.

72. Abbey Foregate 1991. The same area has been a car and lorry park for many years, but interesting schemes for its rehabilitation have been suggested.

73. Column c1860. Victorian visitors were urged to climb the 172 steps of Lord Hill's Column so they could enjoy the panoramic view of the town and the hills around it. The key was held at the Lodge which was lived in for many years by Serjeant Davies who was appointed keeper of the Column at Lord Hill's own request in 1817.

74. Column 1991. The Column was soon surrounded by substantial Georgian and Victorian villas, one of which was demolished when the new Shirehall was built in 1966; this unfortunately also involved the removal of the Keeper's Lodge.

75. Lowcock's Foundry, Coleham 1934. This had been William Hazledine's foundry; Hazledine was involved in many revolutionary civil engineering projects in the early 1800's, but was remembered principally for the ironwork used on the Menai Bridge which was cast and tested at Coleham.

76. Coleham 1991. Only a few of the factory buildings still stand, most of the site being occupied by housing built by 1938.

77. Old Coleham 1964. Mopping up after another flood.

78. Old Coleham 1991. The houses in the distance were built in the 1980s on waste ground which was raised a few feet to avoid flooding; their careful design is in keeping with the nineteenth century cottages which formerly stood on the site.

79. Meole Brace Mill c1920. A water mill occupied this site for centuries, but had been converted to an ice factory and cold store by this date; the ice was needed to store meat, fish and game in the town's shops.

80. **Meole Brace Mill 1991.** The mill and its stream have disappeared. Only a street name reminds us that a mill once stood here.

List of Photographs

More Books on Shrewsbury published by Shropshire Books

Everyday Life in Medieval Shrewsbury, *Dorothy Cromarty*, paperback £6.99
Shuts and Passages of Shrewsbury, *A. Scott-Davies and R.S. Sears*, paperback £2.50
Victorian Shrewsbury, *Victorian Shrewsbury Research Group*, paperback £5.50
Bridges of Shrewsbury, *A.W. Ward*, paperback £5.50

For a complete list of Shropshire Books titles, please write to:
Shropshire Books, The Old School, Preston Street, Shrewsbury SY2 5NY.